MW01012394

IN SEARCH OF GOOD MEDICINE

Hospital Marketing Strategies to Engage Healthcare Consumers

MARK D. SHIPLEY

IN SEARCH OF GOOD MEDICINE:
Hospital Marketing Strategies to Engage Healthcare Consumers

Published by Black Box Press
Troy, NY

Distributed by Smith & Jones

For ordering information or special discounts for bulk purchases, please contact
Smith & Jones at 297 River Street, Troy, NY, 12180, 518-272-2800.
Book design and composition by Sara Tack

Hardbound
ISBN: 978-1-4951-1661-2

Printed in the United States of America
First Edition 2014

For Harold, Jeannette & Dad

ACKNOWLEDGMENTS

There are many people I have to thank for making this book possible. At the top of the list are my thought leadership compadres at Smith & Jones — Alan Beberwyck, Caitlin Mooney, Chris Havens, Lynn White and Sara Tack. Over the years, we have worked collaboratively to schedule, research, discuss, debate, write, rewrite, visualize and ultimately publish our points of view on marketing healthcare provider organizations. It's a labor of love, and one we take very seriously. This book is, in great part, a product of that collaboration.

I also have to thank a few clients, past and present, who have given my team at Smith & Jones the creative license to rethink the status quo and inspired us to do our very best work. These include Anne Armater, Nancy Arena, Jim Connolly, Susan L. Davis, RN, EdD, Richard Henley, Ron Mullahey, Jennifer Susko, Ken Szydlow, Matt Van Pelt and William Van Slyke. There are also many others, too many to mention, who are in the direct lines of planning and delivering quality care who have had immeasurable impact on the contents of this book.

I'd also like to thank my father-in-law, mother in-law and father. It is through their personal experiences with the healthcare system during the later years of their lives, and those of my family members who advocated for their care, that made writing this book no longer an option.

And finally, I'd like to thank those who have chosen the noble profession of healthcare provider — the doctors, nurses, PAs, technicians, anyone else whose job title ends in "-tioner" or "-gist," and anyone who supports them in their endeavors. You are the present and future of the American healthcare system. May we give you the marketing communications tools you need to be the very best at what you do. It's a big job. If we do our job well, hopefully, you can do yours well, too. I, and many others, are counting on you.

Mark Shipley

PREFACE

My biggest fear is growing old and navigating the American healthcare system. I watched my parents and in-laws go through this process, and it was ugly. Because my mom lives nearby, I act as her healthcare advocate. I did so for my father, too, while he was alive, and it's a daunting experience.

Call me selfish, but if over the remainder of my career I can impact the organizations (and their leadership) that have the commitment and the foresight to improve our healthcare system — in whatever form it may take — I will feel like I've accomplished a central mission in my life.

As an advertising agency principal and brand development consultant, I've helped hospitals, physician practices and healthcare networks define competitive market positions and build brand equity. Over the last 25 years, with a few notable exceptions, the healthcare clients I've worked with came to me at a disadvantage to their stronger competitors. What brought us together was their determination to overcome those disadvantages, and perhaps, even outpace the competition.

By studying these organizations' strengths, weaknesses and unique patient experiences, I've learned valuable lessons about the inherent challenges of the healthcare industry and the opportunities to create positive change. Hospitals and practices in this position must approach their marketing with great ingenuity. Strategy has to be differentiating, ownable, relevant and deliverable. In execution, there's little room (or budget) for waste and error. Every single element of a marketing communications plan should contribute to strengthen your market position and elevate your brand. Measure the results of your marketing, then repeat what's working and fix what's broken.

By writing this book, it is my goal to share my collected experiences with today's innovators and emerging leaders, those who have the potential (and the gumption) to change and improve the healthcare system. I hope to inform and inspire healthcare leaders: Chief Executive Officers, Chief Marketing Officers, and members of the C-Suite who aspire to direct and lead their healthcare organizations. All of these leaders need to understand the new marketing model they will need to employ if they want their organizations to be successful over the long-term.

Can a book about marketing change the world? No, but it can influence the important and sweeping change that's taking place in the healthcare industry. By understanding how healthcare consumers' behaviors have changed, and how marketing communications and brand building can direct the conversation with their constituents, healthcare leaders will be empowered to make far-reaching changes in care delivery — both from the top down and from the bottom up. And perhaps, my experience of growing old in the healthcare system of the future will be less frightening than my parents' experiences.

Mark D. Shipley

MARKSHIPLEY@SMITHANDJONES.COM

LINKEDIN: MARKDSHIPLEY

TWITTER: @MARKDSHIPLEY

WEB: WWW.SMITHANDJONES.COM

TABLE OF CONTENTS

INTRODUCTION

WHY WOULD HEALTHCARE CONSUMERS CHOOSE YOUR BRAND?

"We are what we pretend to be, so we must be careful about what we pretend to be."

— Kurt Vonnegut —

Consumers are in search of good medicine.

Today, people in need of healthcare have more options, more information and more at stake, and this is changing the way they choose care providers. Many healthcare consumers, especially younger people, override their physicians referral and look to brand reputation and patient experience when they make their care decisions. They are actively researching their care alternatives to determine how and where they will spend their care dollars.

This is a new reality for healthcare organizations. Hospitals and physician practices are discovering that it's no longer enough to deliver good quality healthcare to remain competitive. To attract and engage these empowered, self-directed patients, care providers will need to maintain a presence in the channels consumers use to find information. They'll need to communicate a distinguishing competitive position: what makes their organization the best choice for care. And, they'll need to deliver their brand promise by aligning their organization to a shared mission and patient experience.

"One-third of hospitals will close by 2020."

That was the subject of a recent email I received from MedPage Today, a provocative and intelligent blog on breaking medical news hosted by Kevin Pho, MD. This email referred to an article written by David Huell and Jonathan Fleece regarding the changing role of hospitals and other healthcare facilities.

Americans connect with a hospital during their most intimate and extraordinary experiences. We are born in hospitals, treated for serious injuries and illness there and, like it or not, we are likely to die in one. Yet, despite a history of "strength and stature in America," assert the authors, the hospital as an institution is in the midst of "massive and disruptive change." There are several significant factors driving this historical shift:

RISING COSTS: Healthcare costs continue to climb, leaving hospitals vulnerable since they are generally the most expensive part of the delivery system. And patients are carrying a greater responsibility for the high costs of healthcare, making them more deliberate with their care dollars.

QUALITY CONTROL: Despite the incredible advances we've made in medical technology, hospital care continues to be relatively poor. Three times as many people die in hospitals from medical errors than die on our highways — 100,000 deaths compared to 34,000. And of those 100,000 deaths, 80,000 are from hospital-acquired infections, which are preventable.

CUSTOMER EXPERIENCE: The average waiting time in a hospital emergency department is four hours. There are not many businesses in America where customers, if offered an alternative, would tolerate this poor level of service.

HEALTHCARE CONSUMERS: Thanks to the Internet, social media and access to information (and misinformation) unparalleled anytime in history, the new breed of patient is better informed, less tolerant, and more likely to seek change. More of us are shopping for and comparing healthcare providers the way we do for other expensive services and products.

As a result of these trends, hospitals will be challenged to compete for market share based on a combination of reputation, quality and cost — just like any other consumer-driven business. Some will fail. Those left standing will enter a new market — the open competitive market — where those who are prepared will rise to the top and those who are not will be forced out of the game. Ultimately, there will be winners and there will be losers.

This book is about the winners.

It's about those of you who 'get it,' those of you who recognize you're going to have to lead your organization into a new market if the hospital or practice is to remain a stable and competitive force. It's about embracing the concept of internal alignment and inspiring your entire organization to deliver on the value promise you are making to your customers: the physicians you support, and the patients and families in your care.

In the new market, you are not 'who you say you are;' you are 'who your customers say you are.'

This book is about true leadership and melding your vision of excellence in healthcare with the needs of the communities you serve. And it's also about presenting expertise, services and philosophy in a manner that helps your organization remain relevant to your consumers.

Will you meet the challenge of competing in the new marketplace?

You can look at the new market in two ways. You can panic (or worse, remain ambivalent) and do nothing, or you can see a tremendous opportunity to challenge the status quo and position your organization as the leader in healthcare for your community – however you define that leadership.

THE CEO'S ROLE
IN HOSPITAL MARKETING

EMBRACING YOUR ROLE AS CHIEF BRAND ADVOCATE

"Leadership determines whether the ladder is leaning against the right wall."

— Stephen Covey —

How one leader's vision changed an organization

A community hospital found itself at a critical crossroads. Closings forced by legislative mandate had left the hospital as the primary caregiver in a small city with two distinct patient bases: a large urban, primarily indigent population, and an equally large suburban, insured population. With a high number of uninsured patients accessing health care through the ER, combined with the hospital's dwindling access to government funding to cover those costs, how was this hospital to remain financially solvent and relevant to both customer segments?

The hospital's CEO understood that his organization's mission was to serve both populations — it was the fixed value in the equation. While the suburban population tended to have high quality care and customer service expectations, the urbanites tended to be the most unhealthy and expensive to treat. He understood that this population was not going to change on its own. How could the hospital shift these high cost consumers away from the most expensive point of entry for care without sacrificing clinical and customer service quality? He had no choice but to reinvent how his organization would deliver care to the communities they serve.

His first priority was to stake out a competitive market position — defining what made his organization's care different from the other three healthcare systems in town. At the time, his was the hospital system in the region with the best clinical outcomes in its primary service lines (cardiac, neuro and cancer). Yet, the competition also had high levels of care — essentially making quality of care parity.

However, what distinguished his organization from the others was its ability to embrace and manage change. It had just been forced into a merger, was smaller and less bureaucratic than the competition, and deep in the throws of reorganization. At a time when public discourse was focused on the problems with our healthcare system, his organization could be uniquely positioned as a leader in healthcare reform — because it was doing it. This became the main theme of its brand message.

His second priority was to begin delivering on this promise. He instituted a system-wide team-building and customer service training program. As his two largest competitors continued to build larger, centralized hospital based services, his organization began moving many services traditionally offered in the hospital out into the community, closer and more convenient to the patients. And it began redirecting the in- and out-patient hospital community toward lower-cost entry points for care, reducing the demand for high cost emergency care and encouraging more preventive primary care services.

His story is just one example of how healthcare leaders can take proactive steps to improve the patient experience and elevate the brand perceptions of their organizations.

Your role as chief brand advocate

With so many employees, doctors, patients and service lines, it's hard to imagine that any system, hospital or practice could create a cohesive and unified brand association. There are literally thousands of ways to deliver the customer experience — and as many ways to mess it up. Yet, top provider organizations have succeeded in creating strong competitive positions that are clear, differentiated and widely understood.

In almost every case I know of, these organizations have CEOs who understand and support the important role marketing plays in the success of their organizations. These leaders champion the position and translate core values from the top-down to every level of staff. People look to the CEO for vision and guidance, as the leader, interpreter and facilitator of a differentiated customer experience. It's from this leadership position that an effective marketing strategy can take root and thrive.

Healthcare CEOs can learn a lesson in leadership from the late Steve Jobs, co-founder and CEO of Apple Inc. His vision for the company served as a guide for making tough strategic and tactical decisions. With such a clear mission, he pursued his vision with confidence, inspired his team to follow his lead, and built one of the greatest corporate success stories of our time.

It helps if the CEO understands what his or her hospital offers that's unique, relevant and appealing to all constituencies. This is the foundation for a competitive position. To realize the full potential of your marketing investment, your hospital must communicate this unique experience, and then deliver it consistently and reliably.

The ability to articulate what makes your organization different simplifies the CEO's job in many ways. It helps your people understand where they are headed and what they need to do to get there. It guides and informs your decision making. And above all, your vision and leadership helps to keep your marketing efforts on strategy.

DEFINING A COMPETITIVE POSITION

UNDERSTANDING WHAT YOUR BRAND STANDS FOR AND WHAT IT DOES NOT

"Great communicators have an appreciation for positioning. They understand the people they're trying to reach and what they can and can't hear. They send their message in through an open door rather than trying to push it through a wall."

— John Kotter —

A tale of two hospitals

I experienced first hand the differences between an organization that shares a common mission and one that does not while dealing with end-of-life care both for my mother-in-law and my father. The contrast in the patient experiences provided by the two experiences was startling.

From the moment I approached the hospital where my mother-in-law was a patient, I felt like I was entering a criminal court. Shady-looking characters and cigarette smokers loitered just outside the front door. Two armed security guards defended the tiny entrance (that had no waiting area), checking ID, photographing visitors and buzzing them through the locked doorway. They didn't smile, say hello, or otherwise acknowledge that we were in a place where people seek care. I completely understand the need for security, but the first impression given by the environment and attitude of the guards was unexpected and off-putting.

Upstairs, on the ward where my mother-in-law was admitted, there was utter chaos, with new bells ringing and buzzers going off by the minute and apparently no one was interested in responding. Clearly the staff couldn't handle their patients' basic needs, much less the more urgent situations they faced. We found that the only way to get care or resolve a problem on the unit was to go to the nurses' station and demand it, which was neither pleasant for us nor the hospital staff.

During the week my mother-in-law was there, we never built a relationship with any of her caregivers, because we never saw the same person again after his or her shift was over. The staff went about their work as if the patients and their families were an inconvenience. They didn't work together to make us feel comfortable or secure in the quality of care my mother-in-law received.

Contrast that with the experience at the hospital where my father was treated. He arrived by ambulance at a chaotic ER, with a lot of activity and people moving around — both staff and patients — but it was organized chaos. The difference with this hospital was that the staff was working together as a team. There was a sense of community around the work and its difficulties.

Shortly after we arrived, the police brought in a man handcuffed to a stretcher. He was apparently having a bad drug experience, because he started groaning and screaming at the top of his lungs. The hospital staff dealt with it by moving him to a private area and acknowledging the imposition on other patients. They addressed the problem in a warm and friendly manner, confiding in us, "You're going through much worse, yet look at how you're handling it."

The staff was polite and respectful even when they had to interrupt our conversation to share information or give my dad a shot. The experience was the same after my father was admitted. The caregivers kept us informed and went out of their way to make my father feel at ease.

My father ended up in ICU, and died two days later. Throughout his final days, his caregivers made sure my father — and our family — were taken care of. They handled problems with respect and consideration. And they never failed to be courteous and attentive.

That kind of professionalism and compassion only happens when everyone understands his or her role in the hospital's mission, understands what's expected, and how to deliver a positive patient experience.

Finding your organization's purpose

Given the competitive markets providers find themselves in and the changes brought on by healthcare reform, leaders must ask themselves some important questions:

- If people can choose where they get healthcare, and they have a bunch of different options, why should they choose our hospital?

- Why should family members want their loved ones treated here?
- Why should doctors choose to practice here?

In the case of the two hospitals in the story above, one had asked and answered these questions, and one had not.

This is the CEO's marketing mission: to bring a clarity of focus about what the organization can offer that no competitor can. You do that by answering one seemingly simple, but surprisingly difficult question: Why should somebody come here for care?

A parity statement alone (Because we're the best!) is not good enough. Not every hospital or practice can claim to be the recognized worldwide leader for their expertise and deliver on it. There can only be one or two in each category that will be perceived as the best at what they do. The Cleveland Clinic is synonymous with heart care expertise; the Mayo Clinic and Sloan Kettering define cancer care. They were the first ones there. It's unlikely that many other hospitals will be able to define themselves in those terms in those areas.

While there are certainly examples of emerging brands taking market share from a recognized leader in other categories (think about how Häagen-Dazs stole share from Sealtest by launching the Super Premium ice cream niche), in healthcare, it's not typically done by going directly against the market. It's done by finding a narrow segment or emotional niche, a different market place that they can command, and then laddering up to compete with the giants. While cardiac, cancer, neurology and emergency services are drivers of reputation, they are only service lines. Sloan-Kettering, Mayo Clinic and Betty Ford Center put all their resources into a very specific delivery system, understanding that there is a trickle down to their other areas of specialization.

Taking a healthcare organization from having no purpose beyond parity and elevating it is hard. That's why so many fail to do so. However, it is possible.

Healthcare and Shoes

The hospital my mother-in-law visited did not answer the important question of why someone should choose their organization, so the employees went about directionless, without a shared purpose or understanding of their role in delivering the (non-existent) brand promise. In contrast, the hospital that cared for my dad ran with a flow that evidenced its understanding of the mission and vision for that hospital, and acted accordingly.

Whether you are delivering healthcare or a retail product such as shoes, you have to have a reason to exist, a shared vision of what you deliver and how you deliver it — and everybody inside the organization must get it.

Take a look at Zappos, the extremely successful online shoe retailer founded by Tony Hsieh. People can buy shoes in lots of different places, why would they do it online (where they can't even try them on)?

The vision Hsieh held for his company was about complete customer satisfaction. By focusing on "delivering happiness" (instead of delivering shoes), Hsieh defines how his organization operates: how employees answer the phone, package and ship their product and handle every imaginable interaction with customers. They did it by creating a service culture designed to make every customer happy. The opportunity Hsieh saw in the marketplace, and what he ultimately focused the entire company around, was in creating a cool, happy and fun way to buy shoes and, yes, to inspire people in the organization to deliver that promise. He hit on something his mall-based competitors could never deliver: going above and beyond expectations to WOW consumers, employees, vendors and partners.

THE LESSON FOR HEALTHCARE ORGANIZATIONS

Healthcare leaders who can embrace this kind of transformative business thinking are the ones who will thrive in the new marketing model. Getting there requires a deep understanding of where you are

IN SEARCH OF GOOD MEDICINE

and where you need to be. What can your organization be the best in your world at? What can you do that is desirable to your customers that none of your competitors can do? What is your focus beyond delivering health care? What makes your organization worthy of surviving past 2020?

What does your organization really deliver?

One way to answer these questions is through rigorous and objective exploration: looking at the skeletons in the closet, patting yourself on the back for the things you do well, and acknowledging the things you don't do well.

It helps to understand your culture, the personality of the organization and the core values you are willing to commit to. Core values are the actions that define a brand, something you're willing to fire an employee over. It's not a core value unless there is a positive or negative result for not living up to it. The positive results for the company are the culture the core value creates, but there is a positive result for the employee as well. The negative is that, if people don't live up to the core values, they don't belong on your team. If you're willing to stand up for core values, then you're well on your way to building a company culture that is in line with the brand you want to build.

Delivering good quality care is not distinguishing. There's a small percentage of healthcare providers that deliver extraordinary care (and a small percentage that delivers terrible care), but the majority of healthcare providers deliver adequate care, virtually undistinguished from their competition.

Take a critical look at your organization

Perform an objective self-assessment of the state of your brand, starting with these questions about your organization, the people you serve and your current position.

ABOUT THE ORGANIZATION

- What are the things you can really do?
- What are the things you can focus on as an organization?
- What are you (what do you do well?)
- What aren't you (what don't you do well?)
- Why did you get into the business?
- Why do you get up and go to work?
- What keeps you up at night?
- Do you have any skeletons in the closet?
- What do your customers think of you?
- What do your non-customers (customers of competitors) think of you?
- How is all of the above different from reality?

ABOUT THE CUSTOMER

- Who are they?
- Physicians who refer?
- Non-staff physicians who have privileges?
- Staff (doctors, nurses, everyone else and their families and friends)?
- Patients (and their friends and families)?
- Donors (why should they give money?)
- What are they all looking for?
- What do they have in common in relationship to you?
- What are the customer touch points?

YOUR MESSAGE - WHAT ARE YOU SAYING?

- Focus - where are intersections?
- What is the one thing we can stand for and believe in?
- What is the line in the sand we won't cross — the flag we will waive no matter what?
- What do we need to keep to live up to the promise?
- Who cares? Is it meaningful to anyone but us?
- What do we need to jettison to make it real?
- Does it help make difficult strategic and tactical decisions easier?
- What is mandatory to keep, even though it makes focus hard?

PRIORITIES? SHORT AND LONGER TERM?

- What needs to happen now?
- What activities will help us gain traction immediately?
- What tactics promise the greatest impact for our investment?
- Who do we need to influence to get started?

HOW WILL WE MEASURE SUCCESS?

- What metrics will prove our results against the goals?
- What tools/systems can we use to measure?
- How will we report our progress?

HOW CAN WE BE THOUGHT LEADERS?

- Is it an area of clinical expertise, or is it an unmet market or emotional need?

Examine the competitive environment

It's likely that your organization competes for the mind of the consumer with a lot of other organizations: hospitals, healthcare providers, insurance companies, HMOs, businesses and practices, free-standing surgery centers, physicians groups and nursing care facilities. In the market I live in, this now includes the local grocery stores, CVS, Walgreens and Walmart. How have your competitors positioned themselves? What are your competitors known for to consumers? How strongly embedded are these impressions and what can you create to find a stronghold among them?

THE COMPETITIVE IDEA SPACE

- Who are your direct AND indirect competitors? (Consider any organization, person or product that offers an alternative to your organization's care)
- When you reverse-engineer their brands, how are they positioning their organizations?
- Are their messages different or the same as yours?
- Are the things they're saying true?

After you've completed this exercise, you should have a clear picture of the competitive idea space. This will help you see where there is saturation (similarity and repetition in messaging) and where there is opportunity (untapped ideas that will help your brand stand out from the background noise).

Getting to a competitive position

So, beyond the quality of care, what does your organization do that's valuable? The entire organization must understand that while we're in the healthcare industry, clinical excellence is only part of what we need to deliver. Everybody — cardiac surgeons, people in billing and housekeeping, the parking garage attendant — needs to understand what makes this place different. You want the garage guy to say something like, "I work in the parking lot of a place that's on this mission."

ALIGNING STAFF
WITH THE BRAND

A SUCCESSFUL BRAND STARTS AND ENDS WITH HOW IT'S DELIVERED

"Basic philosophy, spirit and drive of an organization have far more to do with its relative achievements than do technological or economic resources, organizational structure, innovation and timing."
— Marvin Bower —

One bad apple can spoil the whole bunch

Several years ago a hospital in an affluent community hired my marketing firm to rebrand its organization. It seems the hospital had an inferiority complex; they were feeling dwarfed by several major hospitals in the area. They thought their organization wasn't perceived as "very good" compared to these high-tech and teaching institutions.

They blamed their poor reputation on an incident that happened fifteen years earlier, involving an attending obstetrician who had a baby die during birth. He was charged and subsequently convicted of malpractice. The issue received quite a bit of local and regional press, so the hospital believed it had left a lasting impression with their community and the general perception of their organization.

After conducting extensive research into their reputation, however, our firm found that one employee — a nurse in charge of the ER during the busiest hours of the department — had earned a reputation for being abrupt, impersonal and downright mean to patients and families at their time of need. People felt that her priorities were more important than her patients'. As a result, many people in need of immediate care would drive 45 minutes to an hour away rather than face her in an emergency.

This woman was the first line of contact with the people who came into that hospital. She was their 'community relations person'. And that's how they got their bad reputation. We couldn't find anyone who remembered the obstetrician convicted of malpractice. It didn't show up on our research radar screen at all.

Just consider; one employee out of 2,000 had the power to 'brand' this hospital.

This is what happens when an organization is not clear on their culture, their brand or what they stand for. As a result, it was not clear to employees how they were supposed to serve their customers. There was no alignment with the brand. And if there were a brand to align to, this nurse probably wouldn't have worked there.

COMMUNICATING BRAND
IS KEY TO ENGAGEMENT

A survey of nearly 400 human resources decision-makers conducted by employee benefits provider Unum, in partnership with Harvard Business Review Analytic Services, reports the following regarding staff engagement:

45% said improving staff engagement is a top challenge, and 70% expect that challenge to intensify.

More than 40% said recruiting quality employees is a top challenge, and nearly 60% expect that challenge to intensify.

Nearly 40% said dealing with the impact of health-care reform is a top challenge, and 80% expect that challenge to intensify.

The survey also found that:

A company's values and focus on employee fulfillment are the most important factors in attracting and engaging quality employees.

Being a company that cares about the well-being of its staff was twice as likely to be viewed as very important in attracting and retaining staff as providing a high salary.

An ethical, transparent culture was also more likely to be viewed as very important in attracting and retaining staff over a high starting salary and job security.

This, of course, means that you will need to train your staff on how to transform the vision into their jobs through focused training—preferably by an outside professional, as studies have shown an outside entity is more effective in delivering this type of information.

Your staff represents your rationale and passion for existing — to all the people they know. So, if your hospital employs 4,000 people, that is 4,000 opportunities to spread the word about the quality and commitment of your hospital. And those 4,000 people will tell 8,000 people and so on.

This is part of your plan to leverage the most credible sources. They are a third-party interest with no stake in the future of this hospital other than to continue to keep it running for their future health care needs.

It may be better to communicate a weak brand message than to communicate one that is not consistent with the consumer's experience. It's very difficult to retain customers if, when sampling the brand, their expectations are not met.

That's why internal marketing is so important. Marketing the brand internally is essential to creating the brand externally. The entire team should understand the essence of the brand and know how important it is for them to embody that brand and to be diligent in delivering the brand promise.

Once you have the message, spread it around

Marketing professionals spend a great deal of time and energy establishing brands with advertising that is emotional and beautiful, ensuring every detail speaks effectively to the consumer in just the right tone and style. The question is, however, will the brand promise be delivered when the consumer responds to these advertising messages and becomes a patient? The answer depends largely on whether you have first marketed your brand to your most important audience — your employees — and whether they are drinking the Kool Aid.

There's no way around the fact that before a brand's promise can be sold externally, it's essential to sell and have it embraced internally. At the simplest level, everyone needs to be informed, know the organization's mission and what is expected of them. And you market to every one of them — from your physicians to ER medical staff to nurses, and cafeteria and custodial personnel. Ask for their involvement and listen to their feedback. They are on the front lines and are the people who most credibly and genuinely reflect to the world what your healthcare facility is all about.

EMPLOYEES DELIVER YOUR BRAND EXPERIENCE

To properly deliver on the brand, your physicians, staff and other customers must know the hospital's vision and mission, be able to deliver it and demonstrate it in their treatment of patients and their friends and family — anyone they come into contact with.

All this is part of the stories they tell each other and those outside the organization. By focusing on satisfying and motivating employees, you directly or indirectly create satisfied and loyal customers. In other words, engaged employees mean engaged customers, and more of them. Taking a portion of advertising dollars and redirecting them toward internal marketing facilitates change quicker and helps assure consistency. As far as effective marketing goes, there is no substitute for employee buy-in.

Call it a modern take on job satisfaction; staff engagement is what happens when healthcare employees care about their organization and have an emotional bond to its success.

Employees that feel highly engaged understand and take pride in their roles; they are committed to going all-in to accomplish their goals. Engaged employees tend be a hospital's or practice's best advocates, and the higher the level of engagement, the higher the level of productivity and the lower the chance of an employee leaving.

KNOW YOUR CUSTOMERS

UNDERSTAND WHO YOU'RE MARKETING TO, AND HOW THEY MAKE THEIR DECISIONS

"The aim of marketing is to know and understand the customer so well the product or service fits him and sells itself."
— Peter Drucker —

Recognizing the emotional needs of women

Any time I talk about the importance of understanding your target audience, I'm reminded of a maternity marketing campaign my agency was hired to do a number of years ago for a community hospital. The marketing director expressed concern that their maternity center had seen a steady decline in births in recent years, from a high of approximately 2,600 births to about 1,900 births a year. The decline was the result of women going to competitors for their deliveries.

Part of my client's solution to compete with the trendy birthing centers was to build a new maternity wing, featuring private birthing suites and all the amenities. (One of their main competitors, a birthing center that had taken significant business from them, was located in a double-wide trailer; hardly a state-of-the-art environment.)

My agency was hired to launch a marketing campaign prior to the opening of the wing, to help prevent further market erosion and build census for a successful opening. With their new maternity wing still under construction, we couldn't rely on facility tours or interior photography to attract expectant mothers. What message or strategy would assure the new center a successful launch and quick rise to 100% census?

Our research offered us some key insights into the shift in women's preferences for maternity hospitals. After conducting interviews with mothers-to-be, new mothers, physicians and administrators, we concluded that women weren't paying attention to the building or facility. Women were paying attention to the 'birth experience' and their ability to influence how they deliver their baby.

Think about it. A pregnant woman experiences stressful physical and emotional changes brought on by the progression of her pregnancy. She is likely confused and coping with a lot of conflicting information from all the books she's reading and the unsolicited advice and expertise of her all-knowing friends and relatives ("You're carrying high – it must be a boy!").

Add the challenges of navigating the obstetrics medical process and their suddenly too-tight shoes, and it's no wonder they're feeling out of control. When we feel out of control, we start to look for reasons that we're unhappy and point to the tactile stuff that we can see and touch and smell. Suddenly the wallpaper or the lighting or the bed covers start to matter because of a need to be in control of something.

This insight led us to develop our entire campaign around the idea that mothers-to-be want to feel in control. They want to choose the birth experience that's right for them. And they choose the people (and hospital) who will support their decisions.

Our campaign created a parallel between our target audience's pregnancy and the opening of the maternity center, with headlines such as, "Due (January 2000)" and "Now Showing." Our model represented the stage of pregnancy of our target audience, her belly growing as the center's opening date approached. Subsequent ads addressed their impending delivery more directly, with suggestions like, "Shape your birth experience," and "Fill out your birth plan." The simple calls to action offered informative and interactive tools to help them plan and retain control during their delivery.

The new maternity wing opened to 100% census and needed to expand by an additional 50% just three months after they opened. That year they delivered 2600 babies, a 700-baby increase in one year — a full 36% increase in deliveries.

By knowing the customer, in this case a pregnant woman, we were able to craft a compelling message and images that were relevant to the needs and desires of the customer. Our client was rewarded with increased business and a growing reputation that influences all their care pathways.

Who are your customers?

In most consumer facing industries, the customer is the end-user and payer, with need, want, cost and benefit all part of the purchase decision. Healthcare is completely different, with diverse players and relationships taking on the roles of the customer as the end user, the payer and the decision maker.

PATIENT/CONSUMER AS CUSTOMER: The end-user of the service, patients want everything that could improve or cure their health issue. They want it NOW, because nothing is as important as their well being; AND often without regard to cost since they are not paying for it or, at least, not directly in the case of insurance or government plans. (This is changing with healthcare reform, and consumers becoming part of the cost equation, but this is just beginning to affect their decision making.)

PHYSICIAN AS CUSTOMER: The prescriber of the service, the physician's role as decision maker is rooted in what he or she perceives to be best for the patient, what is medically appropriate (protects them from malpractice), and what is easiest for them to deliver (based on habit or familiarity). Often, this is without regard to cost because they are not paying and are not incentivized to do the right financial thing. (This too is changing, as physicians may be held accountable after healthcare reform, but we don't quite know yet.)

INSURANCE COMPANY (OR GOVERNMENT) AS CUSTOMERS: As the payers (except in cases of elective patients and the uninsured), insurers' decisions are rooted in what is worth paying for as determined by the actuarial analysis of their ROI. And, often the decision to pay for any given healthcare procedure, product, or service is made after the service has been rendered. This leaves you in a precarious position, with some percentage of the product/services you render unpaid for (either refused by the insurance company or government, or simply not paid for by the uninsured consumer).

Understanding the needs, issues and motivations of each of your customer segments helps define your marketing messages and align your communications to each stage of their decision process: including what, where, when and how you communicate with each subset, so they behave in a manner that is financially sustainable to your organization.

Understanding Healthcare Consumers' Generation Gap

The healthcare decision process used to be simple. Patients took a passive role in their care decisions, relying primarily on physician referrals to determine where they went for medical care. But with more care options, changing insurance coverage and a boom in online health information, all that is changing. Now we have a new challenge to think about: marketing to a new breed of 'healthcare consumers.'

Today, patients are shopping for care much the way they do for other retail services. They are actively researching their treatment alternatives to determine how and where they will spend their care dollars.

THREE FACTORS ARE INFLUENCING THE HEALTHCARE CONSUMER MOVEMENT:

• Patients' increased financial responsibility and exposure make them more discerning and deliberate in healthcare decisions.

• Internet access to hospital metrics and physician reviews allow patients to research all of their options, shop based on quality outcomes and get provider recommendations from their social networks.

• Alternatives to traditional hospital care, such as free-standing specialty care centers, offer consumers benefits such as convenience, comfort and cost savings.

This new consumer movement is partly an age-related phenomenon, with changing social habits, technology and information access empowering each new generation to be more self-directed and more independent in their healthcare decisions.

Research suggests that each generation has unique emotional triggers and motivations for choosing care providers, and interfaces with healthcare organizations in a distinctly different way. Here's a look at the values and habits of each generation.

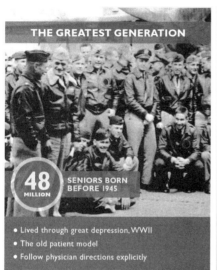

THE GREATEST GENERATION

48 MILLION SENIORS BORN BEFORE 1945

- Lived through great depression, WWII
- The old patient model
- Follow physician directions explicitly

BABY BOOMERS

77 MILLION ADULTS BORN 1945–1965

- Influenced by era of societal change, technology
- Challenge status quo and old models
- Take physicians' advice but research options

GENERATION X

50 MILLION ADULTS BORN 1965–1985

- Lived through cold war, dot-com bubble
- The first true healthcare consumers
- Actively seek information and shop for care

MILLENNIALS

72 MILLION YOUNG ADULTS BORN AFTER 1985

- 'Digital natives' that grew up with the internet
- Shop for healthcare, likely to switch providers
- Influenced by reputation and advertising

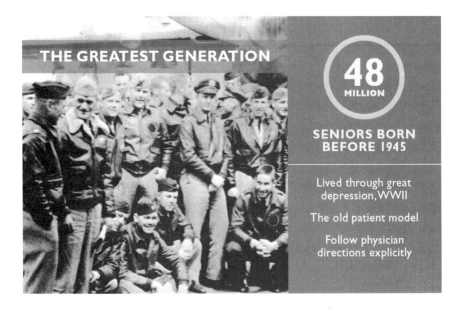

THE GREATEST GENERATION

48 MILLION

SENIORS BORN BEFORE 1945

Lived through great depression, WWII

The old patient model

Follow physician directions explicitly

The Greatest Generation / Silent Generation (age 65-75+):

The Greatest Generation and the Silent or Lost Generation together make up a distinctive subset of the consumer market that clings to healthcare's past and the traditional doctor-patient model.

While people 65 and older make up only 12 percent of the population, they account for 35 percent of hospital stays and 38 percent of emergency medical care. They require more frequent and longer patient visits, and expect a high level of service from their doctors and nurses.

This generation follows doctors' recommendations for their medical care direction, and rely on their physicians for health information and referrals. However, their children — Baby Boomers and members of Generation X — may be influencing or even making their care decisions, often based on their own rationales for choosing care providers.

When selecting a hospital, they're most influenced by where their doctor suggests they go or where they've had prior experiences, followed by the hospital's reputation or its proximity to their homes.

They are the least likely to research health options online or participate in online communities.

MARKETING TACTICS TO ENGAGE THE GREATEST GENERATION:

• Physician referral initiatives: Members of this generation put their care in the hands of their physicians, so marketing to and with referring physicians can be effective in attracting this segment. However, as this aging population declines, and hospitals hire more doctors, this strategy promises diminishing returns.

• The customer experience: Communicating patient experiences, especially when your internal staff and physicians are aligned to deliver consistently positive experiences, is one of the best strategies to attract this generation.

• Reputation building & management: Seniors respond to hospital reputation claims, especially when supported by integrated branding and marketing communications. Because the elderly depend on healthcare, they are open to advertising in mass media, as well as messages delivered within the office environment.

Baby Boomers (age 45-65):

Roughly 80 million strong, Boomers are the leading edge of the 'silver tsunami;' a growing population of senior citizens that is changing the expectations of the healthcare industry. They question the status quo and search for new solutions. In addition to directing their own health care, Boomers are also likely to act as caregivers and advocates for both their parents in the Greatest Generation and for their Gen-X and Gen-Y kids.

This generation is influenced by physicians, but they research their options, challenge assumptions and rely on conversations to make their healthcare choices. Boomers value quality care and consider reviews and rating systems when choosing care providers and specialists.

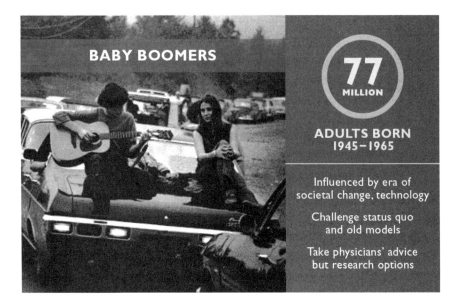

BABY BOOMERS

77 MILLION

ADULTS BORN 1945–1965

Influenced by era of societal change, technology

Challenge status quo and old models

Take physicians' advice but research options

MARKETING TACTICS TO ENGAGE BABY BOOMERS:

• Physician referral initiatives: Because they rely on doctors for recommendations, marketing to and with referring physicians can be effective in engaging Boomer consumers.

• Integrated online and offline messaging that drives to web: Boomers are very likely to seek information online, often in response to TV or other off-line media. 78% of Boomers have searched health information online after seeing something on TV.* Their searches focus on treatments, medications, side effects and risks.

• Reputation building & management: Boomers consider hospital reputation in their care decisions, and respond to integrated branding and marketing communications.

• The customer experience: Communicating patient experiences appeals to Baby Boomers both as patients and as caregivers for older and younger generations. It's important to align internal staff and physicians to deliver consistently positive experiences.

*Source: Google/Nielsen Boomer Survey August 2012

Generation X (age 30-45):

Generation X represents the first generation of true healthcare consumers. Still in their 30s and early 40s, they have yet to create a high demand for healthcare services, but are curious and actively seek information.

Members of Generation X have an affinity for healthcare brands and shop for healthcare much like they shop for retail goods and services. They have short-term expectations of their healthcare provider relationships, and will switch doctors and physicians based on recent experiences, a trait they share with younger Millennial consumers.

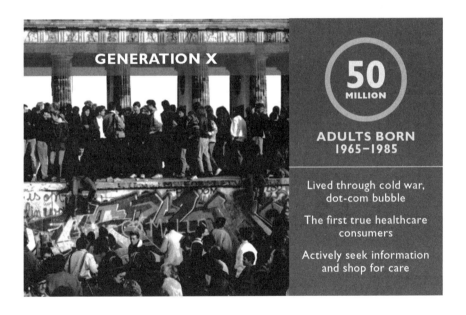

GENERATION X

50 MILLION

ADULTS BORN 1965–1985

Lived through cold war, dot-com bubble

The first true healthcare consumers

Actively seek information and shop for care

MARKETING TACTICS TO ENGAGE GENERATION X:

• Integrated online and offline messaging that drives to web: Gen X patients are only moderately responsive to healthcare advertising, favoring video and in-office messages above other media. They have a natural tendency to consult online information sources, however, so drive-to-web strategies that integrate offline, online and mobile channel messages can connect with the Gen X consumer.

• Reputation building & management: Because they relate to healthcare brands, marketing strategies should focus on hospital positioning, brand messages and positive patient experiences.

• The customer experience: Communicating the patient experience, and aligning internal staff and physicians to deliver positive experiences is integral in attracting Gen X patients. This generation values prior experiences and often consults social networks when making care decisions.

• Physician referral initiatives: Marketing to and with referring physicians can be effective in engaging Gen X consumers, supported by reputation and positive patient experiences.

Gen Y or Millennials (age 20-30):

Generation Y*, also known as Millennials or Echo Boomers (because of the sudden rise in birth rates over Gen X), include more than 75 million adults born since 1982. Only in their 20s, they have low utilization of inpatient and outpatient services, other than maternity or emergency services. They access healthcare mostly through primary care, urgent care and OB/GYN providers.

These young adults tend to shop for and show preference for healthcare brands; they're heavily influenced by great advertising, reputation and patient experiences. Millennials seek information from multiple sources, including online search, reviews and rating sites, their large social networks and word of mouth referrals. They value positive personal relationships with care providers, but they are likely to switch doctors or hospitals if they have a negative experience.

*Physician referral initiatives: Marketing to and with referring physicians, emphasizing reputation and positive patient experiences, influences Millennials as well as older generations.

MARKETING TACTICS TO ENGAGE MILLENNIALS:

• Integrated online and offline messaging that drives to web: Like Gen X, Millennial patients are only moderately responsive to healthcare advertising. Because they are young and healthy, targeting media that delivers messages when Millennials are close to the care decision offers the best results (online, mobile, video and in-office channels). Mobile marketing and mHealth apps fit the Millennial consumer's digital lifestyle.

• Reputation building & management: Millennials show a preference for healthcare brands and creative advertising, so marketing strategies should focus on hospital reputation and patient experience.

• The customer experience: Communicating the patient experience, and aligning internal staff and physicians to deliver positive experiences is essential to engage Millennial consumers. This generation values prior experiences and often consults online information, review sites and social networks when making care decisions.

Adapting messages for the healthcare consumer

So how does this affect your hospital? Advertising your organization's safety and quality outcomes won't attract patients who are shopping for healthcare brands. To remain competitive, hospitals will be forced to focus investment in direct-to-consumer marketing of their 'patient experience,' especially to recruit younger, brand-savvy patients.

HERE ARE SOME OTHER FACTORS INFLUENCING CARE DECISION:

• Location has little impact in hospital selection: Only about 10-12% of all consumers were influenced by a facility's location and proximity to them. People are clearly willing to travel for healthcare, and weight their decisions more on physician referrals, hospital reputation and patient experience.

• Advanced technology only matters for specialty hospitals: Only 10-15% of consumers reported advanced technology as a deciding factor when choosing a hospital, while 70-80% considered it an important reason for choosing a specialty hospital.

• Price plays a new role in care decisions: The rising cost of health coverage has resulted in greater financial exposure for patients, including higher deductibles, co-pays and out-of-pocket costs. In response, they're thinking and acting more like consumers. They're shopping for quality care, but consider value in their decision process. To some degree, hospitals can combat lower-priced competition by building and managing the organization's reputation. Reputation is key because hospitals serve everyone but want to attract the most profitable patients — consumers looking for and able to pay for the best quality care. When care providers compete on price, high-end and low-end providers are well positioned to take market share from those in the middle.

• Online information fuels free choice: Perhaps the greatest change in how people make healthcare decisions is growth in online health-related searches and information resources. Consumers can learn about illnesses, self-diagnose certain health conditions, find treatment options, compare therapies, medications and side effects — all with a few simple keyword searches. Popular review sites such as Yelp and Angie's List offer reviews of physicians and hospitals, and with more than half of Americans using social media, word-of-mouth referrals and recommendations are just a few clicks away.

Prochaska's stages of change

To understand how you can change each customer's healthcare buying behavior — patient, physician or insurer — it is helpful to understand how people accept change. After all, most of what sales and marketing is about is getting people to change: to take an action, to buy something or do something that they haven't done before or buy it from a different person.

One model that I've used to evaluate, track and describe the stage of change is the Transtheoretical Model of Behavioral Change (TTM). Originally developed by James O. Prochaska and colleagues at the University of Rhode Island in 1977, TTM employs different theories of psychotherapy (hence the name transtheoretical) "to assess an individual's readiness to act on a new, healthier behavior and provides strategies, or processes of change, to guide the individual through the stages of change."

Prochaska's model wasn't entirely accepted by academia, but many physicians and marketers have followed it and TTM has remained a prominent model on how people change. As its name implies, it's theoretical, but many in the world of sales and marketing have adopted this (in the shape of the sales funnel) based on the behaviors people exhibit.

FIVE STAGES OF CHANGE IN PROCHASKA'S MODEL:

PRE-CONTEMPLATION – No intention to change behavior in the foreseeable future. Many individuals in this stage are unaware or under aware of their problems.

CONTEMPLATION - Aware that a problem exists and are seriously thinking about overcoming it but have not yet made a commitment to take action.

PREPARATION - Intending to take action in the near future.

ACTION - Individuals modify their behavior, experiences, or environment to overcome their problems, involving overt behavioral changes and considerable commitment of time and energy.

MAINTENANCE - At this point people are working to prevent relapse and consolidate the gains attained during action.

Let's focus on the Pre-Contemplation Stage. The individual has no intention to change their behavior in the foreseeable future, and may be largely unaware of their problems. In healthcare marketing terms, these folks are not currently your customers because they are not in need of healthcare, they're receiving care from someone else, or they don't know they need healthcare yet. Outbound marketing can generate awareness with potential future patients at the pre-contemplative stage.

But the best reason to market to audiences at this stage is that everybody at some point in time is going to need healthcare. Once these folks move to the contemplation stage — where they are aware that a problem exists and are seriously thinking about overcoming it — they begin an active search for information (ideally, your hospital's website, videos or white papers). These are people who are weighing the benefits and costs of behavior or the proposed change. At this point they want more information; they are visiting hospital websites trying to decide which provider or treatment is right for them. As humans, we are naturally drawn to the familiar, and if you marketed to them at the pre-contemplation stage, they are likely to be familiar with you as they move closer to buying.

Understanding how people change will play a critical role in healthcare marketing and will continue to grow in importance in the future as we move away from a fee for service model. This will mean dedicating more marketing resources to getting people to change their health behavior before they get sick (and expensive to treat) through community wellness marketing.

What are your customer touch points?

A touch point is any specific channel through which your customers come in contact with your organization. Individually, that could be viewing a web page, talking to an employee on the phone, or being cared for by a nurse. Collectively, touch points include all of the communication, human and physical interactions your customers experience during their relationship with you. Touch points are important because customers form perceptions of your organization based on their cumulative experiences.

Think about all of your organization's touch points. There are many obvious ones that spring to mind, but touch points are much more than advertising or your website. Touch points include everyone and everything from one-on-one interactions to broad outbound marketing messages. While some touch points, such as mass media advertising, can influence virtually all of your customer segments, each group will have preferred or specialized channels through which they interact with your hospital.

Understanding all the ways your customers interact can help organizations recognize opportunities to improve communications, correct inconsistencies and deliver a better customer experience.

MARKETING TO PHYSICIANS

ALIGNING YOUR BRAND'S GREATEST ADVOCATES AND INFLUENCERS

"When you assume, you make an ass out of u and me."
— Neil Simon —

You're the best at what?

My agency team recently met with a service line cabinet to present an integrated consumer-directed marketing campaign for their particular sub-specialty. Afterwards, one physician asked us what we were doing about marketing to physicians, an issue brought to mind by a recent conversation he'd had. He told us his closest friend, a physician in the same city, was discussing a case and mentioned that he referred the patient to a competitor's hospital.

The doctor sharing this was offended that his best friend had referred to a competitor and asked, "Why did you do that? We've been doing it longer than they have and we're better at it than they are." His best friend replied, "Well, I didn't know that."

The doctor said, "Why didn't you ask?" And his friend said, "It's not my job to ask, it's your job to tell me."

Don't take anything for granted

The situation described above is not uncommon. We work with large physician groups and find that even physicians within their own group aren't talking to each other.

THE 5 DON'TS IN MARKETING TO PHYSICIANS ARE:

1. Don't assume the way things are now is the way they have to be. Practices refer patients all the time, and while they fall into referral patterns, their habits do change based on knowledge about the availability of new services or providers.

2. Don't assume people will go out of their way for you. People make referrals because someone makes it easy for them, not necessarily because it's the best referral. People refer to the leading provider, whether a specialty practice or a huge hospital, because they know the practice's reputation. There is plenty of opportunity and good reason to market your specialties to this audience.

3. Don't assume that the doctor is doing the referring. It may be the physician, the nurse administrator or a receptionist. That person will refer according to what's easiest for them and the patient. Some call for the patient, some let you do it yourself. These things need to be part of the physician marketing discussion. The person scheduling the referral might ask, 'How far do you want to drive?,' 'How early do you want to get in," etc? All these things are driving the referral decision-making process.

4. Don't assume people will remember. If you're not the leading provider or you don't have a reputation as being the top, it's your responsibility to communicate with them exactly what you do. And you need to be able to communicate it to these physicians over and over and over again. Visit or contact them regularly, tell them what's happening, introduce new people and services, send them stuff. Remind them why you can take better care of their patients and make their lives easier.

5. Don't assume reputations are true. Sometimes a doctor is the go-to guy because everyone thinks he's the go-to guy. If you start to look at his outcomes, this may not be true. The guy who's the busiest in town gets the reputation for being the best because he's the busiest – it may not be so. He's actually the guy who's best at building reputation for being the best.

Perceptions, like brands, can have a significant influence on the referral process, so understanding and managing perceptions is important for healthcare providers. I had an interesting conversation on this subject about 15 years ago with a group of cardiologists. One of the doctors drew a simple bell curve to represent all the care providers in the universe.

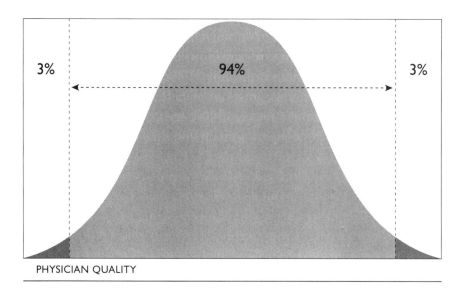

PHYSICIAN QUALITY

He pointed to the small percentages on the left and right, and explained that 1-3% of physicians are terrible and should have their licenses taken away. At the other end, another 1-3% are brilliant physicians, the top of their specialties. In between, there are 94-98% of physicians that are really good, but not recognized as extraordinary or perceived as among those brilliant few.

So how do you get your organization's doctors to be PERCEIVED as among those elite 1-3% that are considered brilliant? Quite simply, you need to get in their faces.

How to market your practice to referring physicians

GO MEET WITH THEM. Give up two patient appointments a month and drive over to their offices and meet with them. Tell them you're making an effort to meet other doctors in the community. Learn about their practice and show how your capabilities can help them care for their patients.

MAKE IT EASY TO REFER PATIENTS TO YOU. Send information to the administrative person on a regular basis. Set up a direct phone line so referrers don't have to wait on hold for 15 minutes. Or better yet, give them a URL and let them go to your calendar and see what's available.

MAKE IT A RECIPROCAL RELATIONSHIP. If someone is referring to you, refer to them. List them on your physician finder and send patients their way when you have the opportunity.

FOLLOW UP ON REFERRALS. Ask referring physicians why they refer to your practice, so you can better respond to their needs and expectations. For example, my agency does routine follow ups to see why physicians are referring others to us for marketing services. This helps us build and manage our reputation and helps reinforce how we both benefit from our association.

MAKE A POINT TO MEET KEY PHYSICIANS IN YOUR MARKET AND INVITE THEM TO YOUR EVENTS. They may attend for networking or professional reasons or just to be social, but it helps build awareness, establish a relationship and position your organization as a professional resource or ally.

HIRE SOMEONE TO PROMOTE YOUR PRACTICE TO REFERRING PHYSICIANS. If it's a big practice, it could benefit you to bring in someone with medical or pharmaceutical sales experience to reach out to referring physicians, nurture relationships and create a presence for your practice, without taxing your clinical capacity.

INBOUND MARKETING

CREATING CONTENT TO HELP PATIENTS FIND YOU

"If you have more money than brains, you should focus on outbound marketing. If you have more brains than money, you focus on inbound marketing."
— Guy Kawasaki —

Getting physicians to the "Aha" Moment

Recently, I attended a physician cabinet meeting to present the results of last year's cardiac campaign and a new campaign for the coming year. Physicians generally support marketing because it helps them attract new patients and hit their quarterly numbers. Too often, however, physicians think that putting their faces on billboards or in print ads is the only way to achieve this goal. I've found that promoting individual physicians in mass media is not only very expensive, it doesn't support the overall brand. I was prepared to have this conversation yet again, when a breakthrough occurred.

One of the physicians spoke up before I even started my presentation. He told his colleagues a story about a patient that he treated on the previous Friday. This particular patient was seeing a cardiologist at a competing hospital and decided that he was unhappy with his care. He went online to conduct a search for cardiologists and landed on our client's website. He was familiar with them from seeing their marketing messages during his pre-contemplative stage. The prospective patient then proceeded to watch all of the physician videos on the cardiac page until he decided on the one physician that he liked best (the physician telling the story, of course). He called the physician's office and was able to get an appointment the next day. Forty-eight hours later, he was at the hospital for a stent procedure and was very happy with his results.

This patient had a completely on-brand experience from start to finish. The marketing may have helped to draw the patient in, but the physicians, nurses and staff all participated in the bigger picture by delivering the experience that the marketing promised. It was great for this group of physicians to hear this tangible and inspiring story from one of their peers rather than listening to 'the marketing people.' And stories like this help motivate physicians to participate in the marketing efforts and act as advocates for the brand.

Content strategies for information-hungry audiences

Modern communications have changed the way patients seek, interpret and use health information to make care decisions. More and more, consumers are tuning out interruptive marketing and instead, actively seeking relevant information through search engines and social networks. Consumers want to know about their health conditions, treatment options and providers, and will engage with brands that deliver the information they demand. Helping them find this information is known as inbound marketing, and leveraging its strengths has become an essential part of an integrated, strategic approach to marketing a healthcare organization's image, brand and service lines. Hospitals and physician practices can use inbound marketing techniques to engage these information-hungry patients and provide a depth of content that traditional marketing doesn't allow.

Inbound marketing is earning the attention of prospective patients by making yourself easy to find and then drawing them in with valuable content through your blog, podcasts, videos, eBooks, eNewsletters, white papers, social media marketing and other forms of content marketing.

Simply put, it means getting found on the Internet.

Inbound healthcare marketing focuses on placing information in front of your prospective customer where they 'live' online and on the platforms that they choose to utilize. These include social media portals like Facebook and LinkedIn, blogs, video blogs, podcasts and a dynamic website. You can also make it easy to find through SEO, keywords and back links. Marketers can use traditional outbound channels (online display, social media, outdoor and even television advertising) in conjunction with inbound to bring traffic to content and help consumers find it faster.

THE MOVE FROM OUTBOUND TO INBOUND

Traditional healthcare marketing (a.k.a. outbound marketing) typically uses one-way, interruptive communication methods such as TV commercials, billboards, direct mail pieces and e-mail blasts. With outbound marketing, the hospital remains in control of the information flow by pushing its messages out to prospective patients in the media we choose. Unfortunately, when used alone, outbound marketing methods aren't as effective as they used to be because today's consumers don't perceive advertising to be as credible or informative as they used to. They are looking for more information and more depth than they can find in traditional advertisements.

In contrast, inbound marketing is the act of creating relevant, credible content, and then helping healthcare consumers find it. It's a difference in how your audience receives your message. Rather than trying to 'sell them' through interruptive messaging, inbound marketing puts the control into the hands of the patient and allows them to find your blog posts, informational videos, and interviews on diseases, treatments, products, physicians, hospitals, and healthy living, on their own terms. Healthcare information is more credible when patients find it themselves, so it makes sense to post it where and when they need it.

ROI OF OUTBOUND VS INBOUND INITIATIVES

Outbound healthcare marketing initiatives are quite labor-intensive, and often have a lower measurable return on investment when compared to many successful inbound healthcare marketing initiatives. In addition, more and more of your customers/patients are online and searching for information about you.

Understanding of the potential of a thorough inbound healthcare marketing strategy, combined with a deep digital healthcare presence, is essential especially to healthcare providers whose marketing budgets are being squeezed on all sides.

Inbound Content Themes and Channels:

THOUGHT LEADERSHIP & EXPERIENCE SHARING

- Blogs, guest blogs and forums
- Position papers
- How-to articles
- Health information

HEALTH & WELLNESS INFORMATION

- Blogs, guest blogs and forums
- Articles on medical conditions
- Treatment information
- Community wellness programs

INTERNAL CULTURE AND PERSONAL STORIES

- Blogs and newsletters
- Physician and staff profiles
- Website videos and interviews
- Social network posts

ONLINE PRESENCE AND SEARCH VISIBILITY

- Online news distribution
- Associations
- Ratings & review sites
- Directories

ENGAGE YOUR SOCIAL NETWORK

- Internal culture and personal stories
- Staff news
- Promote and link to inbound content

An Inbound Marketing Case Study

When we took over the website for one of our community hospital clients, we found that the vast majority people, over 90% of their 22,000 unique annual visitors were coming to the website looking for a job. This was not surprising because, in their marketplace, they're the largest employer. This is true across the United States; in almost every market, healthcare providers are the largest employers.

Obviously, we needed to get people to pay attention to something other than the job listings if we wanted to engage community members and build the online reputation of the hospital.

So we took several things into account.

First, there's just so much information out there. In the old days when there were only three television networks, you could run the same commercial over and over and over again, and get results. People weren't in information overload. Today, consumers are getting hit from all sides, bombarded with messages from their phone, the web, the radio, television, outdoor, print, the list goes on.

Secondly, that it would be nearly impossible to tell the whole brand story and to tell it in a credible way with 30-second TV spots.

Finally, we saw the popular appeal of reality TV. People spend a lot of time hearing other people's stories. They like to hear stories. Stories are very important.

With all this in mind, we decided to build our entire marketing campaign around telling patients' stories. Not just testimonials, having patients say, "Hey, this is a great hospital," but really telling what their story was all about, who they were as human beings, what they were dealing with, why or how they got into their situations, what happened and how they really felt about their experience. These were going to be candid conversations aimed at making an emotional connection with viewers.

We built the entire campaign around these video interviews that were delivered on the hospital's website. We offered patients' stories, and then we added stories of physicians and people that worked in the hospital. And their stories were generally: why did they get into the business? Why did they want to become a doctor? What do they like about their job? And why did they choose to work in this particular hospital?

We promoted the new website and videos with an outbound marketing campaign that invited consumers to come to the website and learn more.

One year later, they had 250,000 unique annual visitors to their website (in addition to the 18,000 people who were looking for employment information), and 90,000 completed video views. A complete flip-flop.

It was a comprehensive campaign to drive web traffic and once they got there, there was content that was 'sticky' — meaning viewers returned to the site, held their attention and spent longer periods of time there.

Getting Found on the Internet

In the real world, patients can follow the arrows on those blue 'H' signs right to the front door of your hospital. When looking for healthcare information online, however, most patients use a key-word search to pinpoint the content that's most relevant to them.

USE KEYWORDS TO MAKE EVERY WEBPAGE A HOME PAGE

Since the most informative and valuable content on your hospital website probably resides deep in your site, these prospective patients are coming in everywhere, NOT JUST the home page. An under-standing of how search engines rank content can make every page an entry point, a search destination that can equal, or even outperform your home page, and drive more traffic to your site.

Search engines review billions of pages of web content to locate the very best information sources. By highlighting what's unique and relevant about each of the dozens or hundreds of subpages on your site, each becomes an opportunity to generate site traffic. Since the top-ranked results on the first page of Google searches usually get 90% of the click-throughs, it pays to refine your content to get every page to rank.

DISTRIBUTING NEWS RELEASES

Another important way to drive traffic is by promoting your content with news releases. Think about Google News and Yahoo! News as different search engines, says internet marketing strategist, David Merman Scott. Submitting news releases can get your content indexed on recognized distribution services to generate alerts and gain potential coverage from mainstream media and bloggers. Including hyperlinks with relevant keywords and targeted pages is essential for search engine ranking. In addition to sending the news release to reputable distributions services, publish a version of it on your own website's media page, blog or wherever appropriate.

CREATE COMPELLING CONTENT

Simply put, content is chunks of information for websites and other online media that is used to capture search engine attention (helping you to be found on the web) while providing information of value to the reader (prospective patient/customer). Today, every business is in the publishing business. Not just thinking or acting like a publisher, but actually being one.

This requires:
- Understanding the personas of your audiences
- Creating content that WOWs both the machines (search engines) and the humans (internal and external audiences)
- Creating calls to action for different stages of the buying cycle
- Distributing content so that it is actually read and found (including social media, email and other channels

or communities)
- Nurturing buyers though the cycle with informative content that gently nudges them forward

A UNIFIED CONTENT STRATEGY

Virtually every department within an organization is creating content in some way. Coordinating it, publishing it and updating it takes tremendous focus and commitment to say nothing of protecting the integrity of your message, as it's handled by so many people. To make content creation as efficient and cost effective as possible, it pays to have a strategy that allows you to easily adapt content and repurpose it for any device or platform.

In their book, *Managing Enterprise Content: A Unified Content Strategy*, Ann Rockley and Charles Cooper give this example:

"Think of a company that sells a software product. They will have product information in a brochure, in press releases, on the web site, on the product package, in the training materials, in the user documentation, and in the customer support materials.

"Now think of how many people created or modified that content, (Marketing, Technical Publications, Training, Web Master, Customer Support).... the cost of translating that content... changing that information three weeks before product launch.... Finally, think of the customer who is receiving all these pieces of information and is trying to get a clear understanding of your product and its capabilities.

"The branding may be inconsistent and the message unclear. Now think into the future when this product becomes just one of many with common functionality across a suite of products and think about how to make sure content is consistent and accurate. The time and cost can be astronomical."

A unified content strategy is a repeatable process that allows you to identify all content requirements up front. Organizations can rely on content being the same wherever it appears, providing both internal and external customers with a consistent message, brand and accuracy.

ENGAGING CONTENT

Professional reputations are important, but social media requires healthcare professionals to loosen their ties a bit. Stiff, impersonal content won't go far on social media. Instead, post information that is conversational and appeals to emotions so your followers will share it with their friends. Think of social media as a place to promote a lifestyle and attract people with similar interests, rather than as a daily newsletter for your organization.

DOCUMENT CHECKLIST FOR PLAIN LANGUAGE

- Written for the average reader
- Uses concrete, familiar words
- Has useful headings
- Uses "you" and other pronouns to speak to the reader
- Uses active voice
- Uses short sections and sentences
- Organized to serve reader's needs
- Omits excess words
- Uses the simplest tense possible – simple present is best
- Uses lists and tables to simplify complex material

Source: www.plainlanguage.gov

Of course, social media is a great place to share information about your hospital or physician group, but content needs to be recreated for this medium. Copying and pasting sentences from your website or donor newsletter into Facebook won't feel genuine. Mix up content with interesting articles you find on other blogs, infographics, recipes and funny pictures. It's okay to make people laugh; you need to come across as human, rather than a robot churning out posts that were preloaded months in advance.

Jeff Pulver, producer of the 140 Characters Conference, said that when he tweets something as simple as "Good morning!" to his followers, he is amazed at the response. Show your human side, which is especially relevant in healthcare, and your patients will show you theirs.

Also, it is important to remember the language gap between the medical professional and layperson. To effectively communicate with people online, whether posting on Facebook or commenting on a blog post, you must use language that the layperson can understand and relate to without being condescending or dismissive.

According to the CDC, research indicates that most health information is not presented in a way that is usable by most adults. It is crucial then for healthcare professionals to write in a clear, concise, well organized way. One of the biggest challenges, particularly in dealing with elderly patients and consumers, is that they don't understand the directions from their physicians. Inbound content also needs to be digestible to the audience you're trying to convince.

Social media posts and webpages that are consistently updated with a fresh variety of content, photos and video can attract followers and bolster the hospital's reputation while sharing interesting information and engaging patients in meaningful conversation.

"By setting a standard of having good patient communication and engaging with patients, hospitals are in fact subtly marketing themselves as a cutting edge institution that offers these advantages," said Nancy Finn, president of Communication Resources and author of E-Patients Live Longer.

SOME CLOSING THOUGHTS ON CONTENT CREATION AND INBOUND MARKETING:

- Objectives. Before you start anything, it's vital that you set goals and develop a plan to know where you want to go. Even though content marketing is becoming a bigger part of the marketing mix, only 38 percent have a content marketing strategy.

• Quality. With content marketing, quality trumps quantity any day. (Read Zen and the art of content marketing.)

• Numbers. People love facts and numbers. And the best content — like the best resumes — include numbers. For example, 91 percent of business-to-business marketers are using content marketing and 86 percent of business-to-consumer marketers are using content marketing.

• Measure. "You can't manage what you don't measure," says the measurement adage. If you fail to measure how well your content performs with your audience, you won't know how well you are doing — or not doing. If you don't have the budget for professional measurement services, you can use a free tool like Google Analytics to determine a variety of metrics.

• Print is not dead. Even though the world is going digital, there is still a tremendous opportunity to connect with your audience via print. (Read 7 reasons to rethink print.)

• Recycle. Since we are all doing more with less, it is important to recycle content and put a new angle on it or freshen it up. (Read 56 ways to reuse content marketing.)

SOCIAL MEDIA

SOCIAL CHANNELS ARE FOR HUMAN CONNECTIONS

"Networking is not about hunting. It is about farming. It's about cultivating relationships. Don't engage in 'premature solicitation'. You'll be a better networker if you remember that."
— Dr. Ivan Misner —

Creating a socially-transmittable brand

As businesses struggle to find their place on the booming Facebook social media platform, my agency is often asked to help hospitals get their head around being 'social.' Part of our strategy is to build a social network from the inside. Let's take a look at one of our clients as an example.

This particular hospital has thousands of employees (and many that use social media everyday). Why not start there, get some percentage of the staff online and engaged, then begin to reach out to staff's social networks?

We recommended posting content that would appeal to their employees — staff awards, honors, community events — human interest stories and things the outside world would be interested in, too. Proud employees shared posts, people congratulated others with a 'Like' and suddenly, they had started a conversation.

We also helped the client create a social media policy on how to reinforce the hospital's brand, take control of social situations, maintain patient privacy and deal with negative comments, and it worked very effectively.

In one year, the hospital went from having a couple hundred followers in their social network to over 3500 followers and hundreds engaging with them each week. The hospital's CEO recently asked us to expand their social activity because, as he said, "We'd rather pay you guys than pay the media." We 'Like' that kind of engagement.

Recognizing social media's true value

Social media is not a miracle cure for weak and underperforming brands and it's not a substitute for an integrated multi-channel strategy. When you understand the channel's strengths and weaknesses, it can become an effective addition to the marketing toolbox.

SOCIAL MEDIA IS SOCIAL, NOT COMMERCIAL.

Social media allows people to easily stay in touch with their friends and family, to make connections with others who share similar interests, and to support social causes and grassroots movements. It helps bring people together and involve them in events much bigger than themselves. It is a social force unrivaled in human history.

Social media is ideal for connecting with those closest to you and working outward. Hospitals have large populations of employees and physicians who together have huge social influence. A message they share may reach thousands, including colleagues, friends and families. Starting your social network with them makes a lot of sense (but raises issues about defining your organization's social media policy).

But the key word here is social: a medium of human connections and interpersonal relationships. It is not primarily a commercial or marketing channel. In most instances, selling is interruptive, even off-putting, so marketers must exercise restraint in driving the sales process. Keep in mind that many of the most popular and successful social media marketing campaigns were movements: campaigns designed to do good and engage people's desire to help others. They were meant to drive traffic but not necessarily recruit customers.

STRONG BRANDS HAVE AN EDGE IN SOCIAL MEDIA

Hospitals, practices and provider networks that have a clear brand position, a well-defined patient experience and something worthwhile to say tend to outperform others in the social media realm. Brands that can connect with their networks, but keep the conversation on a social or entertainment level, are the leaders in collecting fans and followers.

If your healthcare organization has a large base of highly satisfied patients and advocates, social media is an essential channel for customer engagement. Use it to create buzz for your brand through re-tweeting, sharing and linking from your satisfied customers to their friends and followers in the social network. Post health information in Pinterest that people can access and share easily. Word-of-mouth marketing and the opinions of trusted, non-biased consumers carry considerable influence for today's Internet-savvy consumer.

As I said previously, it's inevitable that a small percentage of your patients will be displeased with their experience, and some will express their feelings through social media — especially through healthcare review sites like HealthGrades, Angie's List and epinions. Brands that recognize this can embrace the opportunity to turn a negative into a positive. By monitoring social media conversations for mentions of your brand, you can identify negative comments and make good on patient complaints. This can have a positive rebound effect: demonstrating your commitment to service can turn dissatisfied patients into loyal, repeat customers.

ENGAGEMENT AND SOCIAL MEDIA ROI

'Likes' are nice, but the real goal of social media is engagement — active involvement with the social network in the form of comments, sharing of content and advocacy for the brand. Setting realistic goals and objectives for social media campaigns provide a way to track results and demonstrate return on investment.

And as I've already established, social media isn't free. While the cost of posting content to social media channels is relatively low, the expense of labor to strategize, monitor and engage social networks shouldn't be underestimated. You must consider the costs of promoting the campaign and the time your staff spends on Facebook and Twitter, etc. in project budgets.

USING SOCIAL MEDIA TO SERVE PATIENTS

You are using inbound marketing and social media. Your hospital tweets regularly, engages in conversation on Facebook, uploads videos to YouTube, builds circles on Google+ and even pins photos on Pinterest (more about Pinterest later). However, your physicians should be using social media to connect with patients professionally as well.

According to a survey conducted by Avvo, 73% of patients do their research for physicians online, and a survey conducted by the National Research Corporation showed that 41% of patients search for medical information on social media sites such as Facebook. These patients, now called "e-patients," search for and read patient reviews, disciplinary history, physicians' resumes and published articles in order to make an informed decision, rather than relying strictly on referrals or word-of-mouth.

There is a conversation going on that your physicians cannot afford to ignore

With an online presence, physicians can contribute to this conversation and respond to patient questions, concerns and comments. It is a way for physicians to present themselves as they want patients to view them and their practice or hospital, rather than relying on others' experiences and opinions.

Dr. Howard Luks, a member of the External Advisory Board for the Mayo Clinic Center for Social Media, said, "The most meaningful reason to establish a presence is that patients can find you and perhaps learn a bit more about your perspective, approach and rapport with your patient base."

Utilizing the more popular social media sites, such as Facebook and Twitter, are just some of the ways physicians can connect with patients online. An alternative is participating in Q&A platforms, such as Avvo, that allow patients to post basic health questions, that are then answered by licensed, board-certified medical professionals. Many patients (about half, according to Avvo's survey) turn to online forums before visiting their doctors to gain background information so appointment time is not wasted.

Participating on a blog, Facebook page or Twitter won't prevent patients from making negative comments, but it can minimize and dilute them. Finally, according to Luks, 65% of patients would be willing to switch to a physician who utilizes social media and a strong digital presence can result in up to 15-20% new patients. Clearly, your hospital and physicians cannot afford to ignore this new media.

PROTECTING PATIENT PRIVACY IN SOCIAL MEDIA

One of the biggest objections doctors give for not using social media is that they are afraid of violating HIPAA. Although this is a valid concern, the odds of a physician violating HIPAA on social media are the same as in any other environment, from the hospital halls to a social setting.

HIPAA (in relation to marketing) simply restricts hospitals or physician groups from using private patient information to promote products or services without written permission, and that a patient may revoke a written authorization at any time.

Keeping that in mind, physicians should not talk about patients, even without stating their name, on social networks. This doesn't mean that you can't get inspiration for a blog post from one of your patients, but rather than writing about the patient, make the illness or condition the general topic or subject of the post.

Also physicians should keep personal and private social media accounts separate. You can direct patients to 'like' or 'follow' your professional pages, but do not add them on your personal accounts.

Lastly, sites like Facebook are always changing, especially when it comes to who is viewing your posts. While technically everything you post or write online is considered public, encourage your physicians to pay close attention to account privacy settings, especially on their personal accounts.

A FEW WORDS ABOUT WORD-OF-MOUTH

As discussed in the role of social media and inbound marketing, word-of-mouth is a powerful tool for consumers when choosing a hospital or doctor. Consumer recommendations carry more weight in decision making than any personal research done on the web.

HealthCare Express, a medical practice located in Texarkana, Texas makes word-of-mouth marketing a priority. They use face-to-face interaction to understand more about how their patients heard about them and learned about the practice. Whenever a patient visits the center, everyone is asked how he or she heard about HealthCare Express and most patients say they heard about it through a friend or colleague. HealthCare Express also sends members of their staff out in the surrounding community to network, hand out goodies and visit small businesses.

Word-of-mouth can also be used to strengthen your hospital's current marketing campaign. Baylor Health Care System, located in Dallas, Texas, recently launched twenty-eight 30-second television spots that were patient testimonials and featured them on their website. Since this launch, there has been a significant increase in the number of patients. The testimonials went viral and helped make the center seem more personable, as opposed to 'intimidating' and 'scary.' These testimonials helped change a huge misconception in the brand's image.

To take full advantage of what word-of-mouth can do for your hospital, it is important to create a list of words that you would like people to use when they describe your brand. A word-of-mouth audit (WOMA) can help your communications and marketing team better understand what your patients are saying. It is also important to consistently monitor any social media channels that you are using and monitor what is being said on there.

Word-of-mouth is the best way to understand what others are saying about your hospital and it is important to take the time and listen. In this case, actions don't speak louder than words.

FOSTERING RELATIONSHIPS

According to Peter Shankman, who gave a keynote at the 2012 Likeable Social Media conference in NYC, liking on Facebook and following on Twitter is fast becoming a thing of the past. In the near future, online relationships will work the same way offline relationships do: based on real interactions.

Offline, the concept of amassing hundreds or thousands of names and calling them friends just because you know their names is ludicrous. They have no real relationship with you, no reason to pay attention or care. It's fake and everybody knows it.

Now, if you treat someone nice, do a favor, or share an interest, a relationship could begin to develop. But if you don't nurture it or put effort into the engagement, that relationship will quickly fade.

That's the future of online relationships, too. The more someone interacts with your hospital or practice online, the stronger the relationship will be. Smart marketers are looking for ways to increase engagement and interaction with their customers. This will not only help build the brand but these people will also become advocates for the brand.

Focus on the quality of the engagement, listen carefully to what your customers (staff and physicians, too) want from you to begin the engagement process. Consider what they say and you will build a highly engaged group of brand followers.

KEEPING UP WITH NEW SOCIAL PLATFORMS

Social media is in a constant state of evolution and flux. While Facebook, Twitter, Google+ and Pinterest have proven their sustainability, the next big thing could be just around the corner. My recommendation for healthcare brands is to stay open to new platforms, experiment with new channels and continually test and refine social strategies.

THE MEDIA MIX

DEFINING A STRATEGIC APPROACH TO HEALTHCARE ADVERTISING

*"Half the money I spend on advertising is wasted,
and the problem is I don't know which half."*
— William Lever —

The story of the overexposed surgeon

About a year after 60 Minutes aired a story about how the quality of cardiothoracic surgery programs directly correlate to the number of surgeries performed, we were tasked with launching a new cardiothoracic surgery program. With the quality-to-quantity connection firmly in mind, we knew we needed to create the perception of experience, fast. We had to find a way to make this program seem like it had been around forever and that our doctors had performed hundreds of surgeries. Our message had to say new and improved and old and experienced at the same time. We decided to put a good deal of the marketing budget on establishing this perception.

The campaign featured two creative units with the headlines, "Exceptional heart surgery. No exceptions." and "Need heart surgery? Consider yourself lucky." As it turned out, the new heart surgeon was a pretty good-looking guy so we used a photograph of him in one of the ads. The other ad showed a paid model who looked like Walter Cronkite — older, experienced with a look that just made you believe him.

In the photos, the cardiothoracic surgeon and Walter Cronkite look-alike both had very engaging eyes. You could see them looking directly at you so you had this emotional connection that was important.

We plastered the surgeon's face everywhere and I mean everywhere: newspaper and magazine ads, transit posters, billboards and posters in the exam rooms throughout the hospital. We even bought ads on every single shopping cart in the region, so everybody who went grocery shopping spent 45 minutes with this surgeon's face looking back at them.

About a week and a half after the campaign started running, his wife called the marketing director of the hospital system and asked to cancel the campaign because her husband was getting hit on by women every time he went out in public. Not only was he immediately known as the cardiothoracic surgeon, but he became a recognizable rock star overnight. And the client's fledging heart surgery program gained the visibility and credibility to turn them into a major player in the market. The launch campaign exceeded goals in short order and the client had to recruit a second surgeon to handle the surgical volume.

Two paths to advertising success

CARPET-BOMB: OUTSPEND AND OUTSHOUT THE COMPETITION

The story of this heart surgery campaign illustrates a marketing strategy known as carpet bombing. The logic of carpet bombing is that if you throw enough live ammunition in the vicinity of the target, you might just get the target's attention. In this scenario, we threw a lot of money at advertising in a variety of different ways to hit the largest number of people possible and build awareness very quickly. Sometimes carpet bombing can be an effective way to achieve tactical goals, like in the scenario above. Other times, it can be a considerable waste of money and time.

LASER FOCUS: OUT THINK THE COMPETITION & MAKE PEOPLE CARE

In contrast to the carpet bomb approach, there's another advertising strategy that can achieve similar results, but in more subtle and powerful ways: out think your competition, rather than simply outspend them.

This was our approach to the launch of a successful healthcare network's rebranding campaign. While the competition was spouting statistics and platitudes alongside smiling physicians and nurses surrounded by cold, high-tech equipment, we mounted a web campaign that featured patient stories, told 'in their own words.' Unlike testimonials, these stories captured the patients' emotional experiences when dealing with serious healthcare issues. Naturally, we chose the client's patients, so the client was mentioned. But the point of these stories was not endorsement, but instead to capture the essence of the human condition.

All advertising (TV, print, outdoor, online display, social, posters, etc) pointed to web landing pages with videos of these patient stories. Cardiac advertising sent people to cardiac patient stories, cancer advertising to cancer stories, and so on. The result? More than a quarter million new visitors to the client's website and 90,000 completed video views in a year.

In this situation, emotion equated strength. The honesty of the patient stories, and the emotional connections between the brand and its customers demonstrated the quality of the care these people received. This approach not only drove a high volume of web traffic and video views, it created a powerful presence for the brand in the market, to distinguish it from the noise and clutter of the hospital's competition.

Media Selection: The Changing Environment

The remarkable shift in consumer behaviors was sparked in large part by a revolution in information access and new online communication channels. Rather than relying on physician referrals, healthcare consumers are researching their options and gathering input from a broad range of sources — a hybrid of traditional media, social media and advertising. To reach audiences effectively, it's necessary to deliver messages across the different media platforms they visit each day.

I usually recommend that healthcare marketers build their plans around owned media, paid media and earned media channels. Each of these channels plays a different role in your marketing communication strategy and is perceived in different ways by your audiences.

The "Hierarchy of Media Effectiveness" illustrates the influence of various channels on the purchase decision, from direct personal experience to messages received through earned and paid media. Actual experiences, or first-hand interactions with a brand, have the greatest influence on consumer perception and willingness to choose the product or service. Word-of-mouth recommendations, reviews from trusted sources and news about the brand follow next, carrying greater weight when encountered in the channels the consumer uses daily (such as their social networks). The least effective messages are those delivered through paid media and marketing channels that are interruptive or irrelevant to the consumer's stage of the purchase decision.

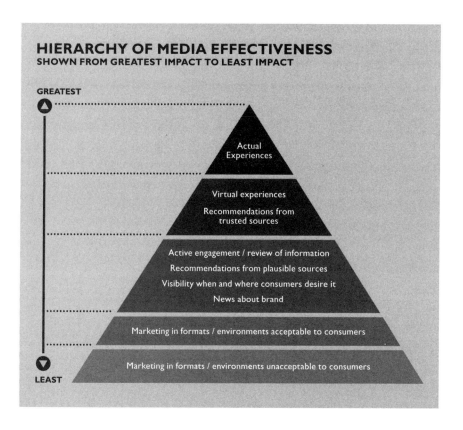

HIERARCHY OF MEDIA EFFECTIVENESS
SHOWN FROM GREATEST IMPACT TO LEAST IMPACT

GREATEST

Actual Experiences

Virtual experiences
Recommendations from trusted sources

Active engagement / review of information
Recommendations from plausible sources
Visibility when and where consumers desire it
News about brand

Marketing in formats / environments acceptable to consumers

Marketing in formats / environments unacceptable to consumers

LEAST

Owned Media

Every day hundreds or even thousands of people pass by your facilities or through your hospital's physical doors. Physicians, staff, volunteers, patients, family members, vendors and other visitors represent a huge captive audience, and an opportunity to engage and inspire them.

However, your physical environment is an often overlooked but highly engaging marketing tool known as owned-media, named so as they represent marketing and communications channels that organizations create or control. They include your building(s) and other physical assets, such as vehicles (particularly valuable because of the exposure they can generate both inside and outside the hospital).

There are endless opportunities to create owned media in a hospital or clinic setting, from external signage, vehicle wraps, art-work, grounds, interior design and digital displays to floor and wall graphics, screen savers, information design and corporate commu-nications. Owned media messages can appear in virtually any public space, from entries to exam rooms, cafeterias to elevators, stairwells to parking garages.

INTEGRATING MARKETING AND ENVIRONMENTAL DESIGN

Finding places for brand messages is easy once you're tuned into owned media. Imagine you're a nurse or doctor on your way to work; look around as you enter the facility, walk down the hallways, or visit the cafeteria. Along the way you'll see blank walls, underutilized bulletin boards, staff memos and posters — each an opportunity to reinforce your brand.

The challenge of owned media is to have an engaging message and mission-appropriate ways to deliver it. Ideally, it reinforces competitive positioning or unique brand attributes. It should mimic the brand, incorporating the identity, color palettes and typography into the environment.

Owned media also requires a careful balance between environmental design and marketing. Health care facilities spend a great deal on interior design. If overdone or poorly executed, it can get in the way of the hospital's mission and credibility and turn the facility into a gaudy billboard.

HERE ARE SUGGESTIONS ON HOW TO USE OWNED MEDIA TO REACH YOUR CORE AUDIENCES.

STAFF: Owned media is a fantastic opportunity to translate brand positioning, share core values and model behavior to consistently deliver the expected customer experience.

PHYSICIANS: Owned media can help cultivate doctors as marketing partners and advocates for the organization. It can align physicians with the mission. In terms of patient referrals, brand advocacy and image, physicians are a powerful group, and one you want on your side.

PATIENTS: Owned media can build long-term relationships by engaging patients and their families who, in turn, promote other service lines and generate word of mouth recommendations. They can become loyal, repeat customers and active brand advocates.

Unlike paid and earned media, owned media delivers relevant content to a highly targeted audience. While the cost of creating great content can be high, so is the return on your investment.

CONSIDER THIS:

- With just limited resources, owned media can revitalize the care environment.
- After the initial cost, it has a lasting impact far beyond most other media choices.

- Owned media reaches the very best prospects and brand advocates.
- Brand-inspired environments can reinforce your position and engage staff.
- Unlike other media, there are no rules, no boundaries and no competition.

Owned media is a blank canvas that can come alive with a little creativity and inspiration. For hospitals and physicians practices, owned media is another tool to support an integrated marketing communications strategy. It's a high-return channel that can be tailored to the core audiences.

Above all, owned media is yours to create, exploit and explore.

Paid Media

While its role in the marketing mix has changed, there's still an important place for paid media channels in an integrated marketing plan. In fact, it appears the big guys — those with strong brands and big advertising budgets — have achieved some of the greatest successes by integrating mass media spending to drive traffic to their social initiatives. The task for healthcare marketers is to understand the intersection of media types and work them in an integrated way.

MASS MEDIA CHANNELS

The golden age of mass media is over, but traditional media channels still work. Print is in a steep decline, but television and transit advertising remain strong, even among young consumers. Audiences are still tuning in; you just have to play to the strengths of the medium. The high cost of mass media real estate and healthcare consumers' increasing skepticism about paid marketing messages limit how much heavy lifting you can do. In most formats, there simply isn't time or space to deliver deep, informative content that consumers want.

As part of an integrated strategy however, mass media advertising can be highly effective in building traffic and audiences for your inbound marketing content. Using short URLs, or links to campaign landing pages, you can use mass media channels to drive consumers to your website or your social channels.

PAID ADVERTISING

Today's consumer has almost total media access, thanks in large part to mobile devices. And paid media is everywhere — on social networks, outdoor and online displays, TV, YouTube, Spotify, Pandora, bathroom stalls, sports complexes, napkins, place mats, direct mail and so on. The task for healthcare marketers is to understand the intersection of media types and work them in an integrated way.

Compared to print advertising, online advertising techniques are relatively inexpensive. Paid search and online display ads provide robust analytics and behavioral targeting opportunities to refine and focus your advertising spend. Based on keyword search phrases, past online behaviors or geographic location, online ad networks can serve your text or banner ads to anyone who demonstrates an interest in your services within your market. To the people being targeted, it will appear that you are spending a lot of money because you will be very prominent. In reality, you will be spending comparatively little because you can target only people interested in healthcare or a specific specialty in the key feeder markets.

Earned Media

Earned media is publicity or exposure gained through non-advertising promotional efforts. Before the social revolution, this meant news stories, interviews with your organization's leaders or event coverage that carries your brand message. The definition has expanded in recent years to include social media, blogs, reviews and ratings. Consumers have become another outlet spreading your message through word of mouth marketing.

This 'viral' aspect of earned media is what makes it such a powerful channel — and one that comes with some risks. Third party recommendations from the press, your patients or their friends and family, are perceived as more credible and transparent than paid messages, but you have little or no control over what people will say through social and news channels. Not all earned media will be positive, but addressing complaints promptly and directly can win back customers and demonstrate your brand's dedication to providing a great experience.

THERE WHEN YOU MOST NEED IT MOST

Every organization will inevitably experience a communications crisis. Taking the time to develop earned media channels — relationships with reporters, blog writers, and broadcast media — can have a huge payoff during a media-driven crisis. While the story will likely still run, your ongoing work could mean the difference between a balanced and fair story, versus one that is biased against you.

Your Hospital is in the Publishing Business

As we put more and more investment in owned and earned media, marketers and the clients they represent have essentially become publishers, spending more of their budget dollars to develop good content and using paid media primarily as a way of supporting owned and earned media.

Ultimately, you want to generate earned media from an engaged audience and create owned content that is distinctive and compelling. To get more attention socially in earned and owned circles, marketers have to have something to say. They have to develop unique, differentiated content.

As I said, being the best is just not good enough anymore. We must make an emotional connection with the consumer. This is the content that tends to go viral and is as viable in healthcare as in any other service.

While it's somewhat easy to imagine a company like Coca-Cola generating earned buzz with a video series featuring amateur athletes, it's more difficult to imagine viral content aimed at patients and physicians. But it is possible.

STAY VIGILANT

IF YOU'RE NOT CAREFUL, IT CAN HAPPEN TO YOU, TOO.

"You're only as good as your last haircut."
— Fran Lebowitz —

The unfortunate case of the misplaced media

Sometimes, context can change the perception of your marketing. Here's a real-world example of media influencing the message: In 2012, a community hospital ran an advertising campaign for cardiology services with unintended results. The campaign featured a billboard with the headline, "Lifesaving Cardiac Care," and the subhead, "Angioplasty with Stenting." While the message was far from compelling due to its heavy use of technical jargon, the physical placement of the message added a sense of irony that was hard to ignore: the small 30-sheet billboard was located directly above a cemetery headstone business. Would you want your cardiac program to be associated with death and cemeteries? Probably not. Check your media placements, and be aware of how context and environment influence your message.

The danger of looking like everyone else

How important is it to make your brand stand out in the market-place? At the crossroads of several major transportation lines and one of the most visible and most coveted outdoor media locations in the market, there were three billboards: one for a bank, one for a college and one for a hospital network.

What made these three billboards remarkable was that they all used the same stock photograph as their main image: a woman with a clipboard. It seems this multifaceted woman was a college student, a bank customer, a hospital patient and an advocate for all three brands at once.

Is it ever a good idea to use an ambiguous, broadly available stock image in a medium where other advertisements run nearby? No. Can original, proprietary images and ideas make your brand different from everybody else in your category and spare you this kind of embarrassment? Yes. Never settle for expected or predictable ideas, and don't let low cost creative solutions water down your brand position. Every message is important, and any one can cause brand erosion.

The risks of using recognizable individuals

Our agency was filming a television spot for a client who chose to save money by casting the talent from staff, patients and other friends of the hospital. At the end of the second day of the shoot, we found out that one of the people who appeared in a key shot was a convicted sex offender. To make matters worse, his photograph had run repeatedly over a six-month period on the front page of the local daily during his high profile trial. How did a notorious sex offender get invited to our TV shoot? The person who cleared him for the shoot was a nun that worked at the hospital. She had forgiven him for his sins and neglected to inform the managing director before the shoot. What she didn't consider was that the general public isn't quite so forgiving, and his image in the TV spots would reflect very negatively on the brand. We had no choice but to hold the crew for a third day to reshoot the scene at great expense to the client.

Would you bring your family to a hospital staffed with criminals? The lesson here is to thoroughly screen any real people — actual patients, caregivers and physicians — to make sure there is no possibility that their likenesses may evoke other reactions than those you intend.

Cheapness never pays

A large cardiology practice hired us to help them build a brand for the practice and improve their awareness and perception within the community they serve. As part of our diagnosis of their situation, we conducted primary research with patients and non-patients to find the source of their less than stellar reputation. Among our findings was that their patients perceived the doctors to be unsanitary.

To save money when they built their beautiful new offices, they elected to put the sinks outside the exam rooms so that multiple exam rooms could share the same sink. Unfortunately, this shortcut left patients with the perception that the doctors were examining them with dirty hands.

From that point forward, these doctors had to enter examine rooms drying their hands without touching anything or anybody until they reached the patient.

On keeping up with the Joneses

A group of physicians demanded a high-visibility print advertising campaign (in addition to the highly effective online display and paid search campaigns) to increase patient volume in their area of specialty. These doctors were particularly vocal and highly influential, so the administration authorized the additional print spend.

A month after the campaign launched, the marketing director checked for changes in volume with the department administrators. It turned out that our online display and search campaign had been performing extremely well and the additional print had little to no impact. In effect, there was no patient volume problem.

The doctors had demanded the print campaign simply because their competitors were advertising in print and they perceived that their hospital's silence in print would result in loss of market share. They were wrong, and the $50,000 that was spent on unneeded print used up precious resources that could have actually moved the needle in areas where need was really present.

This is a clear case for the importance of aligning the entire organization to shared goals and a clear strategy — to avoid unreasonable demands and wasted effort.

THE FUTURE IS HERE.
ARE YOU READY FOR IT?

EMBRACING A NEW MODEL OF HEALTHCARE MARKETING

"If you want to succeed, you should strike out on new paths rather than travel the worn paths of accepted success."
— John D. Rockefeller —

Engaging the healthcare consumer

There's a new reality for healthcare organizations. Delivering quality healthcare is no longer enough. To remain competitive, hospitals and physician practices will need to engage a new breed of healthcare consumers. One that's better informed and more empowered to make their own care decisions.

Hospitals, healthcare networks and large physician practices will be forced to compete in an open consumer-driven market, whether they like it or not. Their leaders and decision makers will need to understand the power of a differentiated brand. It's imperative that they communicate it both internally and externally, and align their staff to deliver a positive patient experience at every touch point. Successful healthcare marketers will embrace new communication channels chosen by the consumer, and find genuine, authentic ways to build relationships and offer value.

This new market presents a tremendous opportunity to position your organization as the leader in healthcare for your community. I hope you'll be inspired to take action and work with others as we reimagine healthcare for future generations.

FURTHER READING

This book represents a snapshot view of healthcare marketing at the time of its publication. Healthcare is in the midst of massive disruptive change, and the way we market healthcare organizations is adapting and evolving. New ideas and technologies, like CRM and PRM, are just beginning and will continue to impact how we engage healthcare consumers in the future.

If you'd like to stay abreast of the latest thoughts and developments from a management perspective, I invite you to subscribe to the following:

PROTOCOL
The Marketing Report for C-Level Hospital Executives and Practice Administrators
http://smithandjones.com/journals/hospital-marketing-newsletter/

HEALTHCARE MARKETING WHITE PAPERS
Timely, in-depth papers on macro topics that inform anyone who is involved in or can influence healthcare marketing decision-making
http://smithandjones.com/journals/healthcare-marketing-white-papers/

THE HOSPITAL MARKETING BLOG
Timely updates and information on micro topics anyone involved in healthcare marketing should be aware of.
http://smithandjones.com/journals/healthcare-marketing-blog/

ABOUT MARK D. SHIPLEY

Mark is on a mission to help improve the American healthcare system. During his 25+ year career in brand development, he has played a leading role in discovering and implementing brand building programs for hospital systems and large physician practices.

He co-founded Smith & Jones in 1985 with his partner Sara Tack. Under his direction, this firm's work has won Best of Show in the Healthcare Advertising Awards, as well as being recognized by The Aster Awards, the American Marketing Association, One Club, New York Festivals and The London International Awards.

Mark serves on the Board of Directors for the Albany chapter of Entrepreneur's Organization, Troy 20:20 and YMCA Camp Chingachgook, is Past-President of the American Marketing Association of New York's Capital Region, and a board alumni for The Eddy (the long-term division of Saint Peter's Health Partnership), The Arts Center of the Capital Region, Beginnings Day Care Centers and The Hunger Action Network. He is a frequent guest lecturer on brand building at colleges, universities and business organization events.

Mark studied psychology, sociology and communications at UC/Boulder, advertising at FIT and advertising copywriting at the School of Visual Arts.

In his free time, Mark is an avid bicyclist, traveler, skier, hiker and kayaker.

Mark D. Shipley
MARKSHIPLEY@SMITHANDJONES.COM
LINKEDIN: MARKDSHIPLEY
TWITTER: @MARKDSHIPLEY
WEB: WWW.SMITHANDJONES.COM